Deserts
of the World

Written by Keith Pigdon
Series Consultant: Linda Hoyt

WorldWise
Content-based Learning

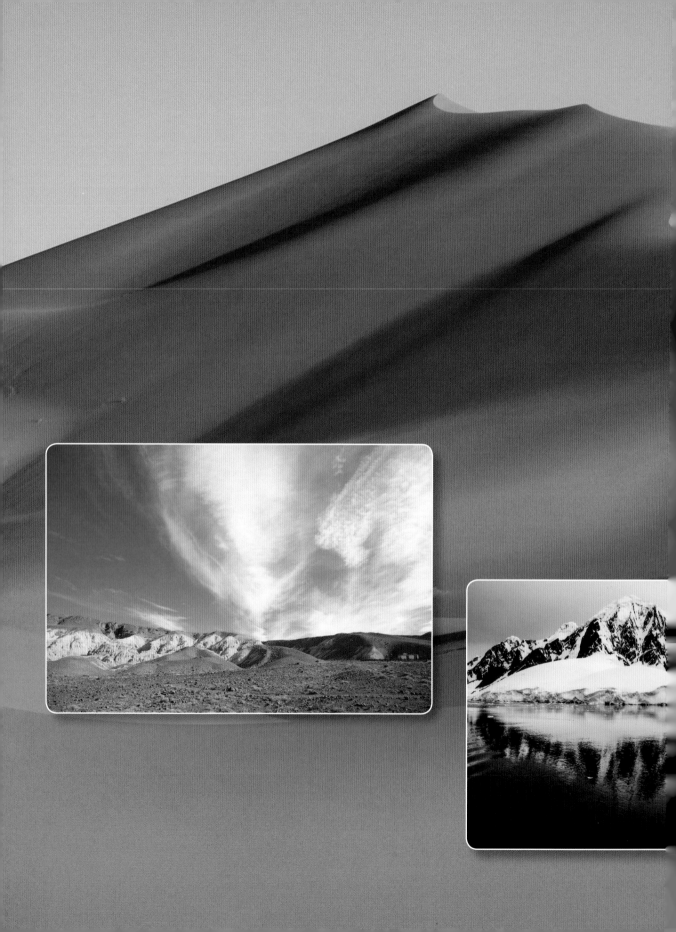

Contents

Introduction

When you think of a desert, do you see a sandy, hot and dry place? If so, you are not the only one – because that's what most people think.

But there are different types of deserts around the world. Some deserts are very hot during the day, some are hot in summer and cold in winter, and there are other deserts that are always very cold.

These deserts might be different, but they all have one thing in common – they are very dry places.

In a desert, it does not rain very much or very often, and life is difficult for the animals and plants that live there.

Chapter 1
The Sahara Desert

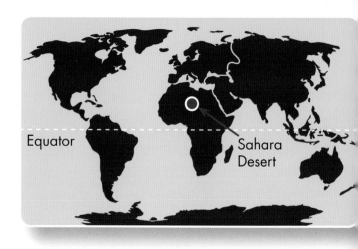

Equator

Sahara Desert

A hot desert

The Sahara Desert in Africa is the world's largest hot desert. Hot deserts are found near the hottest part of the earth.

Much of the Sahara is rocky and flat, but in some parts, there are large, rocky mountains.

The hot, dry winds that blow across the Sahara slowly wear away the rock and turn it into sand. This sand is blown by the strong winds into hills called sand dunes. Often, these sand dunes are what people see in their minds when they think of deserts.

At night, when the sun goes down, the Sahara becomes very cold.

Living in the Sahara Desert

Palm trees grow near waterholes and rivers in places where there is water.

Most parts of the Sahara have very few plants. How do they survive?

Some of these plants store water in their thick stems to use when it is dry. Others have long roots that spread to reach water. Many of the plants have small thick leaves. Smaller leaves lose less water.

Some animals such as camels and goats feed on plants, eating the seeds, leaves or flowers. Birds such as finches and owls feed on plants, too.

Some animals are hunters that hunt animals found near the plants or in the sand and rocks during the day. Other animals such as lizards and owls hunt their **prey** at twilight or night, when it is cooler.

Find out more

Find out which animals feed on plants and which hunt animals to eat.

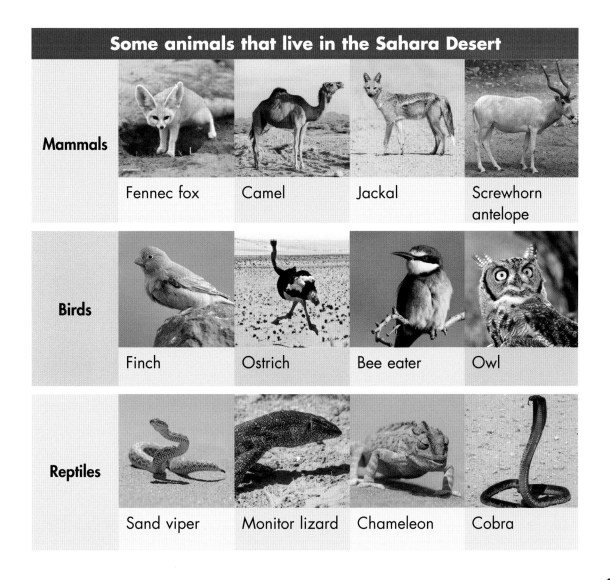

Some animals that live in the Sahara Desert

Mammals	Fennec fox	Camel	Jackal	Screwhorn antelope
Birds	Finch	Ostrich	Bee eater	Owl
Reptiles	Sand viper	Monitor lizard	Chameleon	Cobra

Chapter 2

The Gobi Desert

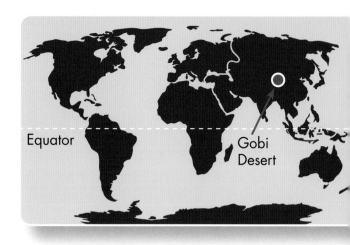

Equator

Gobi Desert

A cold desert

The Gobi Desert is a cold desert. Cold deserts have long, hot, dry summers, and freezing winters with very little rain.

The Gobi is between the Himalayas, the highest mountains in the world, and the ocean. But it is a long way from the oceans that could bring rain.

There are mountain ranges, sandy **valleys** and rocky valleys in this desert. During the cold and dry winters, the ground can be covered with snow.

Did you know?

The word *Gobi* means "waterless place".

11

Living in the Gobi Desert

Several kinds of bushes and herbs grow in the Gobi Desert. One small tree collects and stores water underneath its bark. Animals and people use this water when other watering places have dried up.

The saxaul tree stores water underneath its bark.

Some animals that live in the Gobi Desert

Mammals	Przewalski's horse		Snow leopard	
Birds	Golden eagle		Demoiselle crane	
Reptiles	Central Asian viper		Plate-tailed gecko	
Invertebrates	Desert tarantula		Scorpion	

There are only small numbers left of most of the animals that live in the extreme **climate** of the Gobi Desert.

Three of these animals are endangered:

- Snow leopards are endangered because they are hunted for their skins.

- Gobi bears are **critically endangered** because there is now less rain, and less food for them. There are only about 20 bears still living there.

- Przewalski's horses became extinct in the Gobi, but they have been bred in zoos and are now being brought back to the desert.

The remains of many kinds of extinct dinosaurs are found in the Gobi.

Grey wolf

Ibex

Magpie

Vulture

Steppe rat snake

Mongolian toad

Ant

Centipede

13

Chapter 3
Antarctica

A polar desert

Antarctica is the largest desert in the world. It is a polar desert, covered with ice and snow, and is always very cold.

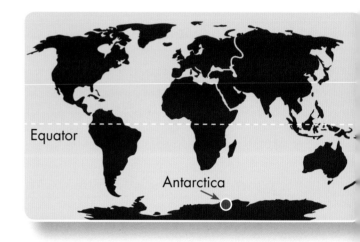

Antarctica has very little rain each year. A huge
amount of water in Antarctica is frozen in sea
ice, **glaciers** and **icebergs**, but plants and animals
cannot use this water to live.

Living in Antarctica

It is almost impossible for plants to live in Antarctica because there is not much water or sunlight, and the temperatures are freezing. It is also hard for plants to grow, because they cannot get enough food from the soil.

Only three kinds of flowering plants live there. (One, pictured here, is Antarctic hair grass.)

Large animals can live in Antarctica, but they cannot stay for the whole year. Penguins and other birds spend part of the year on the land to breed and raise their young, but they spend the rest of the year in the water.

Some animals that live in Antarctica

Mammals

Elephant seal   Leopard seal   Whale   Dolphin

Birds

Emperor penguin   Wandering albatross   Skua   Tern   Gull

Invertebrates

Krill   Mites   Worms

Conclusion

Deserts are places that are always changing. Strong winds and very high or very low temperatures make life difficult for the plants and animals that live there.

But living things in deserts have special **features** that allow them to survive in these places.

Glossary

climate what the weather is usually like in a place

critically endangered has an extremely high risk of dying out and becoming extinct

features the parts of a living thing

glaciers very large sections of ice that are slowly moving

icebergs large pieces of ice floating in the ocean that have broken off a glacier

prey an animal that is caught and eaten by another animal

valleys the low, flat areas of land in between two hills or mountains

Index